ELITE TRADING TACTICS

ELITE TRADING TACTICS

ARIA NIGHTINGALE

CONTENTS

CHAPTER 1

Introduction to Day Trading

Introduction: Day trading is the act of purchasing and then selling a security within a single business day. The primary benefit of engaging in day trading is the potential for significant, short-term profits. However, it cannot be denied that day trading requires the investment of a considerable amount of time and effort. Day traders spend a great deal of time monitoring securities and prices for potential investment opportunities.

They work in a fast-paced environment and act swiftly to realize these profits. While investors and other financial professionals share the same goal of financial success as day traders, the process of day trading is much different. Day traders make and lose a lot of money every day. A common misconception is that day trading is similar to gambling. While many consider the fast-paced nature of day trading to be exhilarating, it is essential to understand that successful day trading is not a result of luck or chance, but rather from an effective trading strategy. There is also a significant amount of risk associated with day trading. By learning about the following terms and concepts, you will be further prepared to ultimately understand a variety of elite trading tactics used by professional day traders.

Defining Day Trading

Day trading is essentially a term that often gets diluted in the investment community because it is so frequently used over time, especially on online trading platforms. When people hear the term day traders, too often they believe this means the trader must close their position at the end of the trading day, or perhaps the end of the week. A trader is not restricting themselves to a strict 9:30 to 4 trading day by any means. Also, a day trader is clearly and simply not a long-term trader. They are simply focusing on short-term, intraday fluctuations that occur in the stock market and more worldly with and focus on intraday price movement.

Our Elite room is and will always be about day trading, plain and simple, but within that denotation, there are a few prominent distinctions. If you are a long-term trader, don't sweat it! It's just as difficult as being a day trader and because we started out trading longer term so we have the knowledge and resources, if you need, to help you begin in your trading education. With our twenty years of experience, we will work with all levels of traders and help you to generate cash flow in the markets, regardless of the type of trader you are, or want to be. To sum up, a day trader buys and sells many stocks per day and makes an intricate and front-loaded box that costs more to labor within and the transactions pay point of sale income taxes. It is acceptable to equity for small industrial-sized traders.

Benefits and Risks

Several reasons can make you want to join the trading world - day trading, to be precise. Here are some of them:

◈ Huge profits: Day traders can make quick profits due to the short-term trades. ◈ Physical work location independence: Access to robust internet connections can make day trading possible from any place in the world. ◈ Work schedule flexibility: Day traders can trade whenever and wherever they wish. ◈ Part-time employment is available: Day trading can be carried out as a part-time job. ◈ Costs of courses, data feeds, software, and a new computer with multiple monitors. ◈ Getting in on the wrong side of a big move. ◈ You will make mistakes and shortly realize how much the mistake costs. ◈ Day trading can take a good chunk of your time if not all. Success has a price. ◈ Commonly, even on a good trade, trading commissions, ticket charges, and minimum investment amounts will eat up a large portion of your profits. ◈ Fear and cost of losing out to better trades or not making any. I had this for the first month.

Day trading typically provides a string of good days (both emotionally and financially) and then a string of bad days. Not everyone is really ready for the minimal or zero wins. Each and every trade is irrationally important for the emotionally fragile person. After a string of a bad couple days, day trading is not for everyone ready for measuring in larger time increments. A string of a bad couple days - while minimal or zero wins are likely every day - can devastate them. Intra-day and day-to-day fluctuations are important, but larger moves need not as much monitoring. It also requires a bigger trading pool to enter larger moves, so I will not discuss this.

CHAPTER 2

Understanding Market Fundamentals

Understanding market fundamentals is important because many of the economic indicators that traders focus on when developing their outlooks can influence price movements. A price represents the optimal consensus that could be agreed upon between buyers and sellers, taking into account all of the good and bad news, in addition to their expectations. When there is a shift in the balance of goods and services, as well as their respective expectations, such as near a top or bottom of a cycle phase, price might represent a suboptimal value. As a result, prices frequently move back to a more equitable value.

Another habit of the market is to provide certain strategic opportunities related to psychological transaction handling. For example, when the price continuously fails to exceed a significant high, traders get nervous that the price will reverse. Many will be triggered to close their buy order, including those traders that bought after the consolidation phase in expectation of a breakout.

Moreover, there are other market dynamics driven by the supply/demand imbalances. Prices often go too far from the average price and the release of new information. Every trader can have an acute awareness of general, recognizable, or identifiable market trends or patterns. However, each trader can realize some level of fear distortion when faced with the need to execute trades with an unknown outcome. Fear of taking a loss is often cited as one of the primary reasons for losing trades being held until a profit is lost or a larger loss is mysteriously discovered later. Market trends and patterns tend to transform over short periods of time as new information is discovered. Many of the reliable but oversimplified trading notions suggest that traders buy low and sell high. Yet, it's often a lot harder to do than it sounds. Moreover, unless a trader is in a market with very strong sustained trends, buying low and selling high aren't enough.

Economic Indicators

There are many metrics and indicators that influence a trader's approach and sentiment. With that in mind, there are several pieces of information or updates that can have a significant impact and fall under the category of economic indicators. Here are just a few of those indicators and the role that they play in the day trading landscape.

These economic indicators are essential for day trading. As such, it is crucial that traders are aware of the days and times that these reports are being shared. In addition, it is also important to understand not only what each of these reports covers, but also how the market may interpret and react to the data that makes up these economic reports. This understanding can lead to slightly different decision making around the time when these reports are released. A key benefit to trading economic indicators is that this type of trading does not require continual monitoring during the trading day. These trades can be scheduled for a predetermined time of day around the release of the report.

Market Trends and Patterns

Price action generally experiences directional movement across various time frames. This directional movement in prices is also often accompanied by the development of recurring formations in market behavior, which are often represented in price charts. Each specific pattern formation or chart pattern is simply descriptive of price movement in response to economic or fundamental data and news. While this type of information on market trends and patterns is interesting, it is the ability to anticipate price movement based on market trends and patterns that is of paramount importance to the day trader.

Any day trader must be able to determine the market's overall direction and the major intraday price activity. This is important because: the major trend will tell the trader if he should concentrate his efforts on the long or short side of the market. He can use a certain technique more intelligently and effectively if it is in harmony with the market's major trend. It is critical to the evaluation of both the psychological data and the chart formations that a stock be first appraised to determine the major trend. Without considering such evidence, a trader runs the risk of taking a position in a stock that is counter to the major trend.

Stocks do not move higher or lower in a straight line but tend to experience times of quiet, steady accretion or distribution, followed by sharp directional movement. The behavior of stock prices leaves imprints on the charts that can be identified and interpreted. A complete understanding of stock price trends and the various waves of market price action is a key to profitable trading. Traders may capitalize on these chart formations that signal the ebb and flow of crowd sentiment, as well as news-driven fluctuations in intrinsic value on which they may capitalize.

CHAPTER 3

Technical Analysis

any day traders adopt a two-pronged approach to trading, using both fundamental and technical analysis. Technical analysis is the study of market action, primarily through the use of charts. It is based on the theory that prices on a chart cover every single piece of fundamental information, plus any outside market factors which have an effect upon prices. If market conditions change, the chart will change. Technical analysts claim that how a market behaves is more important than why it behaves that way. In short, technical analysis is the manner in which any of us can crunch the market numbers in a statistically-accurate way to determine what the likelihood of something happening in the future will be given the current market numbers we are looking at.

The market price is discounted and the chart is a graphical representation of sentiment. The market corrects the price that the majority have judged, which is why it is best to know regarding the minority of professional traders who are the elite few using charts, to give a head's up before the market begins to move into correction. Today's high is the previous day's low, so trading styles and beliefs are many. All schools of technical analysis have developed from the same universal laws. Elite traders must have a true understanding, and this will bring control, which will in turn help in reducing stress.

It is important when one is studying or engaging in trading of the market shares to incorporate the techniques. Know what the charts are saying, understand the dynamics of options and futures markets, find leading market indicators that bring confirmations. Additionally, always consider the markets as a barometer for geopolitical and world events. You will then know why world markets are acting the way they are.

Chart Patterns

A chat pattern is a visual representation of historical price movements of an asset, as depicted on a price chart. Traders hope to use these chart patterns as an indication that collective psychology toward an asset may be on the cusp of a change in direction. The most powerful part of using chart patterns, along with indicators, is that traders can measure historical completion rates to give them an indication if it is statistically worth it to take a specific trade. For day traders, it is good practice to look for chart patterns in five-minute, one-minute, 30-minute, and hourly charts. This will give a trader an understanding of the short-term trend (1 and 5-minute), with the longer-term hourly chart to filter out some of the 'noise' in the two lower charts. If you put the chart patterns from all of the different timeframes above on your chart, you will have a holistic view of the asset in a top-down approach.

There are chart patterns that represent a potential continuance in trend and chart patterns that represent a potential trend reversal. Knowing the difference is crucial to be able to set the correct risk versus reward trading situations. A continuation pattern suggests that the price movement in an asset that we have been seeing will remain the same with the current trend resuming its direction after a period of consolidation. A reversal pattern tells us that the upper hand between demand and supply is reversing, leading to the possibility of a new trend beginning. This new trend could be the start of a positive or a negative price movement.

Indicators and Oscillators

There are a multitude of indicators available that can give you an eclectic mix of information concerning market oscillations and price behavior. Because the market doesn't oscillate as the indicators imply, there will be whipsaws where the orders are given by the indicators and the market gives out a contrary signal. As a result, we perhaps should only rely on the direction the market is going at the time our trading signal indicator is forecasting a profitable entry point or exit point. Indicators and oscillators are used by day traders to help them have a better probability of making a profit. They are able to forecast the short term movement of a currency in a 5, 10, or fifteen minute window. They are in place to help determine the right time to buy or sell a security.

Such use of the oscillators is good in a swing-market. This market will not have as many whipsaws or retracements and will be a good trade in a system like this. But in the near term trading market it would have too many false entries and thus could give a bad investment. The best indications to make a good decision are the candlestick indicators. They forecast much better than the other indicators. In this market, the assets are flowing out if the candlestick forms against the prevailing trading. Likewise, during a down trading market assets will move up against that trend if the candlestick formation indicates the trend is about to reverse. Doing this type of indicator reading will give the day trader a much better chance of making a good investment. No matter what type of system you use, be careful and safe in your trading. Remember that the market is a two-way street; everyone is risking their cash. Prevent pouring all of your money into one position and manage your margin account with care.

CHAPTER 4

Risk Management Strategies

One of the most important aspects of day trading activities, and trading in general, is the risk associated with price movement. While there may be a large upside on any given trade, there is also considerable risk that trades can move against you and diminish the value of your trading capital. Thus, managing and mitigating risk is one of the core components of day trading futures and other trading endeavors. Here are a few of the strategies which most professional traders have developed and use when considering their position sizing:

Don't risk more than 1% to 2% of capital on a single trade. By having and implementing this rule, you eliminate the possibility of one large loss wiping out multiple profits. A short-term trader is looking for ten or more ticks in the trade or about $125 in profits before considering the trade. Consider reducing to one contract per trade for accounts between $3,000 and $4,500. The reasons for developing this rule are as follows: - Reduced exposure to trading losses: By trading fewer contracts, a trader may be able to reduce the emotional attachment associated with trading an account and thus further diminishing the chances of panicking and closing out a trade early. - Gives you the opportunity to adjust to the learning curve of day trading. Use a stop loss that is based on price action and specific structure found within the trading system and represents the price at which your trading analysis is no longer considered valid. Many traders are taken to long-term gains by using a daily support and resistance area or level for stop placement and not actually placing the stop market order at the area.

Position Sizing

Importantly, powerful though these statistics are, they can break down. If a trend turns into a nasty blistering bear, there's no point talking about how the futures did between 1971 and 1999. Thousands did not use this information to their advantage during the 1929-1932 massacre, either. That those were sharp, dear bear markets. Futures trend followers will have such disasters, too. The 73-75 downturn took quite a chop out of them too. According to legend, Curtis' company lost around 80-90% of its customer equity in early 1975—the biggest so-called drawdown ever. This might just be urban mythology, or exaggeration.

So, always tabulate the maximum hypothetical drawdown that would have obtained historically. Then add 20% to it. Assume something similar could happen in the future. At that 120% of worst outcome, decide whether the futures-trading pattern of yours still seems so compelling. Remember that 120% of the worst drawdown is an absolute floor for the potential maximum drawdown. If that sum is comedy-book material to you, chances are you do not really understand the level of risk involved. Position sizing is the art of adjusting your trade size to control that level of risk. Without position sizing, trading in a leveraged instrument such as a futures contract can be as reckless as betting it all on one spin of a roulette wheel. Position sizing means assigning to each trade not just an exit-loss, but the appropriate trade size.

Stop Loss Orders

By far the most important thing you can learn about day trading profitably is how to protect your capital from significant loss in the shortest time possible. Protecting your capital and managing your losses is the most important aspect of day trading. If you are a winning trader at the end of the day, the week, or the month, the net result is all important. How much money you make and how much money you lose overall are key to success. For example, in swing trading, one can have as low as a 40% success rate in trades and still be very profitable. The key to achieving this is to limit your losses on your losing trades and allow your winning trades to gain maximum pips.

Stop loss orders display solid discipline, and this gives you an edge over traders who don't use these orders. Good money management teaches that you should always have a predefined target of when you will exit a trade. The stop loss order is the single most useful tool for keeping your losses small and controlled. Stop loss orders really come into their own when a trade goes wrong, causing significant loss. In the long term, cutting losses quickly and running profits artistically through the use of trailing stop orders has proven to be the most profitable form of trading. Remember that stop loss orders can be used as urgency orders when something significant is likely to happen in the market. A stop loss order in this case is used to protect your profits, not limit your losses.

CHAPTER 5

Developing a Trading Plan

We have talked about trading psychology and execution tools. I want to begin drilling down on the process of developing your own game plan. To me, nothing is more fundamental to success in the market than a clearly defined trading plan. A trading plan is a comprehensive mosaic that defines a trader's dealing system, main goals, the market in which he wishes to operate, his methodology, his risk tolerance, and money management rules. It can be as simple or as complex as you wish, but just be assured that it becomes so fully detailed that you have to rely on it as a trader in order to help make every decision you create in the market and the order to execute. A trading plan essentially supplies an absolute semantic card for you to deal in.

The initial point you need to know when formulating your own trading plan is simply what kind of day trader you would like to be. Everyone must develop their own strategy or a combination of any of these strategies to fit your own time hypothesis, the repertoire that you manage, and the risk disposition which you will afford your position to take. The following segment gives an account of the kind of trading perspectives and day traders. This provides you an idea about how to create your trading plan.

Setting Goals and Objectives

As a day trader, the market demands a lot from you. The pressure of financial commitments and the aim of personal development are also crucial aspects of the trading world. Focusing on your goals can help you navigate your approach to success and direct your thoughts and actions, keeping them in line with important things. It takes bravery, humility, and trust to set definite trading objectives and goals. These are the values that need to be nurtured in order to begin the development of both. Just with a really strong trading strategy, developing worthwhile trading objectives necessitates planning.

Undoubtedly, the biggest reason to set goals involves ensuring that you possess objectives and aims that are both measurable and specific. If a goal is not specific, then it is easy to have a justification to fail or to subconsciously diminish its value. A specific goal consists of a time limit, a price point, and a vehicle. Importantly, it should also state the reason that endpoint is desired. It must be measurable and give the trader a clear yes or no indication of the state of the goal. It is not enough to want to be happy and wealthy. As with your broader life goals, it is important you reflect on the attractive characteristics of success and wealth in your trading for you.

Creating a Routine

Trading can be approached in numerous ways, but there is a significant advantage in having a structured routine for trading. A daily approach to trading is effective because the markets change every day and many opportunities arise during the typical trading day. As financial markets evolve, consumers will likely have access to these markets in new ways. Therefore, as a day trader, you will frequently need to change the time of day or platform that you use to effectively trade. There are a variety of ways you can make an impact in the day trading world.

The daily routine is the process of putting on trades and doing market maintenance during the day. It is reported that the daily trading routine is the most important aspect of trading. The routine can be as important as having a good trading plan. If you lack a good trading plan and a good daily routine, it can significantly improve your trading. Without consistent application of your trading plan and trading routine, maintaining discipline becomes a challenge. You plan to perform market analysis as an effective way to bring structure and rhythm in your daily trading routine. While every hour does flow into the next when markets are moving in a directionless fashion, you should be constantly following a rhythm or a signal of change in market flows because it shows you and is a free signal to be alert.

CHAPTER 6

Psychology of Trading

It is said frequently that the most important component of trading is the psychology of trading. What does that mean? This refers to two parts. One is the emotional side of trading: fear, greed, anger, etc. The second part deals with cognitive biases. It has been proven that our minds are rife with biases that don't serve us in times of uncertainty. The first part, emotions, is actually very easy to control. All it takes is to 1) develop a set of rules that will serve as a guideline for all trading decisions, 2) actually follow the rules.

The 15th century philosopher, Leonardo da Vinci, is said to have said "When the imagination occupies all my thought, it looks much less upon defect." In trading, that means: do not worry about the P&L (profit and loss)! Looking at the P&L can create emotional perturbation, fear when losing much money and euphoria for winning a lot of money. Both of these emotions can lead to the improper execution of systems. This is hard to actually make work; otherwise, everyone would be making tons of money trading the markets.

The second part, cognitive biases or MRIs (mental roadblocks for investing), is about recognizing when you've fallen prey to one of the shortcuts and made a trading decision based not on an objective system, but an emotional feeling. These are sometimes hard to see and harder to stop. There aren't many traders who started early in their lives trading the markets that can overcome all of their biases. The trick is to learn to see these after the fact, see where your feelings might be influencing your decision, and try to learn how to overcome them the next time.

Emotional Discipline

Emotional discipline is critical, especially for day traders. In financial markets, a trader must make split decisions depending on significant data, news, price, and stop points, which are continually fluctuating due to changes in supply, demand, and market order flows. Do you think you have what it takes to receive margin calls, issue stop orders, and execute a profitable trade with a rational standpoint? It's simply a matter of managing your responses. It works similar to an athlete, and in this instance, your opponent is the trade market.

The following strategies are recommended for maintaining emotional composure: - Believe in the concept of getting better 1% each trading day or function. - Analyze trading decisions made by excellent traders to examine your thought processes. - Set both long-term and short-term trading targets and always complete what you started. - Consider acceptance as a perfect peace of self. - If a trade demands immediate attention, consider taking a walk. - Set boundaries and stick to them. - To build an increasing familiarity with the markets, perform a slew of paper trades. - If the markets cause too much panic, relax. - The trading screen should be kept as clean as feasible. - Be concerned about such severe losses, but don't obsess about any one market. Instead, commit to remaining effective.

Cognitive Biases

Cognitive biases describe the psychological dispositions or individual prejudices that we have. The term even says prejudice - assessed against something. The goal of analysis is to name the most important "weaknesses" and to reduce their impact. The advantage of analysis is that deficiencies are determined, the level of their impact is indicated, and counteracting or minimizing the impact through self-control and composition of investment sessions is suggested.

Regardless of the markets you invest in, investment strategy or time frame of your investment, you will always be influenced by emotional and irrational factors. People are more driven by emotions and instincts than logic, and therefore the investor is very susceptible to making investments under the influence of emotions. The influence of emotions occurs no matter if you buy the stock of a large corporation or speculate on the futures market. Understanding these biases and implementing appropriate solutions to counteract them should be a priority separate in the workplace.

Overconfidence in trading can exacerbate psychological biases which may lead to faulty decision-making. The first element to improve is learning; seek out new sources of knowledge and try to evaluate the validity of that knowledge. Learn about cognitive biases and you will begin to understand the irrational side of your own decisions. Risk management is the next crucial skill. Plan each trade with a specific entry and exit, and stick to it. Do not deviate from your plan. Keep a trading journal and function by the numbers. Trading will teach you more about yourself and your limitations, but also offers potential for personal development.

CHAPTER 7

Advanced Trading Strategies

After an extensive discussion of the vital set of knowledge and skills, the basics which every trader should practice and master, it is just appropriate to advise you day traders that it is about time to introduce more intricate ideologies and advanced methodologies. In essence, all trading strategies are for the purpose of taking advantage of the market's undulation, and as market trends dictate the record, trading strategies are contingent upon trends.

If you would like to do momentum trading, which is one form of intraday trading technique, what you need to have is a position in the market. In order to take a trade, you begin at the market open, and you exit your position when your target is met, which could be either at the end of the day or at any time that your trading objective is fulfilled. But the thing is, what do you say if the price of the day's market did not near the anticipated price, leaving you without any trade? A sophisticated approach that suits some traders is contrarian trading. This plan is based upon the theory that the success of intraday trading is heavily dependent upon the ability of a trader to spot the footprints of the predominant money flow or trend and effectively trade it.

Momentum Trading

Introduction: Momentum trading is often positioned as the most profitable and simplest of all trading strategies. This is because the primary focus and essence of momentum trading is to look for stocks that are either going up or down pre-market or stocks that are continuing after the market opens. These stocks should have a relative volume above 1 to ensure profits.

There is generally a lot of noise in the stock market, and it is reasonably difficult for day traders to differentiate between stocks that are actually moving and news-related gimmicks that make stock prices look like they are moving. It is thus important to filter out the news-related gimmick stocks from those that are actually moving. The approach is to develop a stock trading system that specifically targets and aims to justify the real opportunities (the actual movements in stock prices).

Theoretical concerns: The main problem of trading in general is diminishing returns. The reason for this is that trading cannot create an opportunity, but rather it tries to exploit an existing opportunity. Thus, by following or chasing too many people, we lose the edge that we thought we had. Instead, our main aim is to enter when the volume is backing our move and to exit when challengers begin to contest us.

Contrarian Trading

Contrarian trading is based on the belief that the prevailing trend in stock prices may not always be the best guidance for investors. Most of the time, prices reflect investors' expectations of a company's future earnings and are usually correct in their estimates. However, sometimes expectations are unrealistic and prices go beyond what they should. This could happen in both uptrends and downtrends.

It is exactly when prices have gone way too far that contrarian investors find opportunities in the market.

However, the fact that a stock is overbought or oversold may not always be the perfect timing indicator. That's why it's always good to couple these tools with other indicators. For example, overbought stocks followed by topping patterns, resistance, or bearish candlesticks are better short candidates than the former. A key point to make is that no system will ever time the market perfectly, getting in close to the bottom and out close to the top when purchasing stocks. It's through experience that a trader gets better over time at isolating extremes. It's when the risk/reward proposition seems very much in your favor that you have to pounce. As a trader or investor, always check the fundamentals of a company before taking your positions. Fundamentals include the company's profits and whether these are on the way up or down, in relation to the stock's current price and PE ratio.

CHAPTER 8

Utilizing Technology

- Utilize technology. - Imagine the earliest stock market traders and how they operated compared to modern-day traders. They certainly did not have access to the wide variety of technology that is available today. Mobile devices, particularly smartphones, provide access to numerous tools and resources that can be useful for day traders. - Trading platforms: Disconnects in the late 1990s led exchanges such as the Nasdaq to offer electronic trading. Referring to trading done via computer or smartphone, electronic trading connects investors to a wide range of trading platforms. There are also trading tools that can be purchased as or within the trading platform. - Transformation to Algorithmic Trading (AT): Day traders can and do use AT, but the greatest percentage of AT is utilized by institutional traders. First, a computer program must be created to execute AT trades. These computer programs operate using a wide range of complex algorithms. AT is also used to calculate trading parameters. These are the numbers that are used to trigger buying and selling in AT. Time-Weighted Average Price (TWAP) is an example of a trading parameter. When an investor uses TWAP, there is an AT calculation to measure the average intraday trading price and provide a benchmark to trade around. The concept behind such a trade would be that if that average price were one dollar, trading at one dollar and five cents would be a good buy point. Also, every stock transaction must be benchmarked to provide the investor a measure of trading performance. Technology has made it possible for computers to measure the performance of other computers, such as TWAP trades. AT parameters can also be traded against one another. For example, an investor can use VWAP against Volume Participation ("piece trading"), compelling firms to look for participants in similar strategies. The whole consideration of trading strategies and timing should take into consideration the many trades competing against one another since time is the third dimension of this 4X problem.

Trading Platforms

A trading platform enables traders to exchange paper assets and cash in a financial market. It further provides necessary information, such as updated quotes, maps, and other financial data. Almost all trading is performed electronically, which allows it to be carried through smart devices and home computers. Electronic trading is availed through an electronic trading network. The public may use several electronic platforms, which generally need to be paid a fee. Websites are the only form of interface for many electronic trading networks. Others offer computer applications, whereas any type of platforms have both interfaces. In international markets, traders initially send instructions to trade through their personal computers, cell phones, and other devices.

Once these orders reach the electronic trading network, they are then directed to the final market. People considering capitalizing in the stock market should cautiously conduct their analysis of the various trading platforms available to them. Several parameters relate to the platform. The operational tool available to the user contributes to their knowledge. Subsequently, success is likely to be a reflection of knowing how to use what one possesses. The trading platform is a primary trader's tool, and traders need to know how to make the best of it. Besides, markets are very volatile, and that involves changes in tables, direct access to executing trades, handling restrictions, tracking of timelines for real-time data, and lots more.

Direct Access or Web-Based

There are two different types of platforms with online brokers: direct access and web-based. These platforms give the power to directly exchange an electronic trading network, pay either per trade, per share, or contract fees. In all cases, as an advisor, subscribers must pay. Network membership means quick execution, accessing one or more NASDAQ agents, level II presentation, and ECN charges. However, behind the direct access brokerages are sometimes large expenditures. A new trading platform designed to offer advisors an online commission-based service, including tutorials, trading tables, real-time quotes and news, is a web-based trading platform. Only after execution the NYSE, AMEX, and a selection of NASDAQ, OTCBB, and Pink Sheet stock trades will cost you nothing.

Algorithmic Trading

Algorithmic trading refers to the use of programmed software, known as trading algorithms or automated trading systems, to automate one or more aspects of trading, such as order generation, automatic trading, and order management. Such systems are commonly used to manage investments across various asset classes and trading strategies, from those focused on short-term trading to those focused on end-of-day strategies. This field is also known by other names such as black-box trading, robotic trading, and automated high-frequency trading.

Algorithmic trading can be used to automate a variety of trading strategies, such as momentum and statistical arbitrage, mean reversion, and trend following. However, this publication uses the term "algorithmic trading" to broadly cover the entire technology used in trading systems where there is an element of automated order generation or electronic trading. This paper's focus is primarily that of an end-of-day trader seeking to automate their trading strategies, the decision-making process, trade agreement, and order execution. Nevertheless, for the purpose of providing one key insight to the reader, the publisher has discussed high-frequency trading practices in the stock market, as well as the effects of directly crossing and engaging with HFT strategies.

CHAPTER 9

Monitoring and Evaluating Performance

Monitoring and evaluating performance are essential for a day trader to assess the efficacy of their trading approach. This chapter focuses on assisting day traders to be disciplined and effective at monitoring and evaluating their performance. It covers how to keep a trading journal, how to use performance metrics to evaluate results and decision-making.

The trading journal is an important tool for all traders to keep. It requires discipline and honesty in order for it to be worthwhile. The trading journal should be clear and uncluttered. The journal should detail the type of trade, trading vehicle, entry, stop-loss, profit target, reason for shutting down the trade, outcome of the trade, chart for each trade, and comments around each of these metrics. This data is used to inform consistent mistakes and good habits, and to create self-awareness around typical errors and positive decisions to implement focus. It is very much a performance feedback tool. Traders should also be tracking and regularly reviewing trading metrics in a post-trade review analysis. This review will provide information around potential edge in the market, consistency and performance feedback, personal statistics, recognize personal biases, and assess risk and money management based on previous stats.

After each trading day, the last 4 trades of the day need to be broken down into metrics. These metrics are used to measure performance in various corners of the trader's decisions. Results should be recorded in a "violation report" and reflect the movement and buy/sell boxes closer to the current price depending on where the trader entered and the direction they traded. The spreadsheet then needs to be set up to analyze metrics. For instance, a trader can set the time, quantity, and average price where each trade is recorded, and the metrics are then auto-filled when these figures are input. Every trader should aim to have their statistics at these levels: percentage of winning trades (Win%), best trade, worst trade, average net points per trade, maximum adverse excursion, maximum winning trade, and total number of trades.

Keeping a Trading Journal

The benefits of journaling: It's important for day traders to record their activities and decisions during the trading day as well as in the post-trading day analysis time. This is because day traders must act quickly and be decisive—losing time doubting oneself during active trading can result in losses. However, carefully considered decisions and changes can improve trading—or at least reveal the errors from which traders can learn. Keeping a trading journal is an essential part of facilitating trader analysis, allowing for a detailed evaluation of both successful and unsuccessful practices.

Creating a journal may seem time and labor-intensive, but the process is well worth the effort if substantial profits are users' goal. Traders who choose to create and maintain a trading journal can expect the following results: Identifying mistakes and good decisions, boosting mental health during trades, facilitating backtesting of new strategies and tools, proving one's successful decisions to doubting friends and family, and demonstrating traders' unenthusiastic results to doubting friends and family. The act of recording the trading day's events can note actual rather than subjective results, showing a clear picture of trading strengths and weaknesses. By reinforcing or ruling out potentially profitable decisions, even new traders can greatly improve their trading strategy by daily journaling. Rookies and seasoned traders alike are sure to benefit from diligent, accurate, and specific journaling. With a few pen strokes and the click of a mouse at the end of each day, users could already begin honing their strategies toward consistent profits.

Performance Metrics

Performance metrics are used by day traders to quantitatively assess trading performance. Metrics should be created within the context of the trader's goals, detailed trading strategy, and the market traded. Clearly, it is impossible to achieve top performance in every area, so traders will also want to identify which metrics are most important to the performance evaluation of their particular trading. This can help them with identifying what issues may be affecting poor performance.

The win ratio is the number of winning trades divided by the total number of trades. The P&L per trade metric divides the total P&L by the total number of trades. The result is the average amount of P&L realized with each trade. Some metrics to help convey the relative safety of a system are variance of P&L and average adverse excursion and probable adverse excursion, which measures the average amount in the red, and an investor can expect to decrease to a specified level of confidence x% of the time. The average win ratio and average P&L per trade are typically used to determine both the achievement of these goals and the consistency with which the trader can meet these goals.

The win ratio and P&L per trade measure the frequency and magnitude of a curve in terms of tops and bottoms. To say the least, any of these performance metrics on their own may not give traders a true gauge of how a system has been performing, which is why all three or four should be used, if possible. If any metric is performing poorly, it may be more correct to form a generalization regarding how well the system is operating. For instance, if a system has an above average win ratio but poor P&L per trade, the trader may deduce he is taking profits too early.

CHAPTER 10

Adapting to Market Conditions

Adapting to market conditions is an essential skill for day traders. In a perfect world, the stock market would follow a consistent pattern or rhythm called momentum. An upward bias in the market, followed by pullbacks, and back to upward momentum is the ideal environment for stocks - something called a bull market. When stocks fall, everything falls. This opposite movement is a bear market. Of course, the day trader wants to focus on their long and short opportunities, where you can make money regardless of the general stock market direction. In less than ideal environments or general momentum markets, day traders do better when they attempt to trade volatile stocks. Consider employing a strategy that matches the trading day's volatility so that you can make consistent profits.

When initiating a trade that can close open positions in minutes or hours instead of days, weeks, or months, you are a day trader. The term "day trader" is vague, and it can mean anything from a person who careers $500 in a number of small trades to a high-speed algorithm capable of completing 500 transactions in five minutes. Therefore, the main characteristic of a day trader is not a specific strategy.

Rather, a day trader is a person who values speed. Having the capability to insert and remove securities as quickly as possible not only means higher returns but also implies lower commissions. Platforms charge on a per-trade basis or, even worse, a spread which generates fees on every trade in and out of the market.

Bull and Bear Markets

There are two distinct periods in the market – bullish and bearish. Bullish periods are characterized by higher prices and investors holding a primary position in stocks or buying them. Conversely, bearish markets are marked by lower prices and most participants holding a short position, which is when you borrow and sell a futures contract at some point and buy the same number of contracts back at some point in the future.

Bull Market When the stock market is experiencing a bull market, it means everything is in good shape generally. Notably, the economic situation may be good, and companies are posting regular profits. Fear is absent from the general investment community, as investors are likely to close more long positions and potentially open short positions. It is during these bullish trends that institutions and establishments are also buying new assets. Buying trends start to spread quickly. Generally, the market rises continually before experiencing a temporary shift where profits are taken and the lower priced laws may take time.

Bear Markets A bear market is a period of contraction in the economy and the securities market. Many people cannot afford new goods or perhaps do not expect corporate profits to be beneficial. This results in falling stock prices. However, the term 'bear market' is a bit apocryphal, as bearish days are often seen as higher market returns. Simply put, while most of the profits are being harvested for the defense of the circumstances, the slow thinking of long-term renting goes down. Perhaps even the short players prefer to remove their funds due to geopolitical issues caused by fear. Finally, stock returns slowly drift lower and lower. As more and more occupations await the next improvement, they begin to feel the hopelessness and despair of the other stages of decline.

Volatility Strategies

Volatility strategies are trading tactics designed to capitalize on market movements once they occur (or protect against them). This style of trading operates on the assumption that increased volatility comes from news. Increased panicky volatility can make an apparently wayward market run for enormous gains. It can also make a trend look like a breakout ready to roar.

Low Volatility Strategies Check that the short-term low volatility is part of a longer-term market's normal behavior. Periods of low volatility can signal times of climax buying or selling. The market will roll, drift or range in a legitimate buy or sell case. The markets can only trend a maximum of a third of the time.

Author's Response: Yes. Most markets in cryptocurrency and Forex are prone to trend only 20% of the time. This leaves a lot of time for ranging markets. My goal is to break down the best ways to profit or protect from each category.

High Volatility Strategies or News Trading The news (fundamental analysis) is what changes perception (technical). Be ready. If habitually trading while the news is released, it is strongly suggested you open a demo account for at least 3 months. Then, trade the news using this system: Buy-Sell RSI. In other words, buy when the RSI is less than 50, and sell when the RSI is greater than 50. Look for either extreme level on the RSI for a non-traditional system. This approach will focus on news trading. After the news is disseminated, one of three scenarios will take place. Market opinion is varied, and the market will subsequently rally and rise. The market starts to rise on the news, then falls quickly. Internet buying quickly ignites a massive short covering rally. Any news released after a very bad or very good news situation occurs will not influence price movement greatly. The squeeze or fear buying/selling has already begun. The continuation of this earlier situation will resume.

CHAPTER 11

Regulatory and Compliance Considerations

Trading is heavily regulated to ensure fair and orderly markets, to protect investors, and to avoid any potential scams. As a day trader, you'll be best to adhere to these regulations to avoid potential legal issues. The U.S. Securities and Exchange Commission (SEC) is the main regulatory body regulating securities firms in the United States, as well as U.S.-listed stocks, options, and other exchange-traded products. However, the Financial Industry Regulatory Authority (FINRA) and MSRB also regulate trading in securities. It is your responsibility to know and follow the laws regarding such trading in your jurisdiction.

When you make a profit, you need to pay taxes. The profit you will make on your day trade will be earned as a short-term gain, so the tax rates on those profits will differ from the regular income tax rates. Always check with your accountant and the local tax authorities to ensure that you are abiding by all of the tax laws. Here are some of the details you should pay attention to for tax purposes: Non-professional traders are subject to short-term capital gains and other taxes instead of the 60/40 capital gains scheme. The proprietorship method redefines income for traders as a small company owner. Traders who opt for a defensive mark-to-market account measure can lose the 60/40 split favor trading financial instruments. We aren't offering tax advice here. Consulting with a tax professional that understands your individual situation is the best course of action.

SEC Regulations

Understanding how rules and regulations shape broker-dealer relationships with clients is the initial step in being able to succeed as a day trader. One overarching regulatory scheme that impacts broker-dealer and investor relationships is the federal securities laws (securities being stocks, options, bonds, and other financial goods that must be registered with the Securities and Exchange Commission—SEC). The Securities Act of 1933 lays out the basic registration requirement and invest with due diligence principle. The Securities Exchange Act of 1934 extends these responsibilities to on-going dealings in securities and focuses on broker-dealer and market behavior. The concept of a "security" is broadly constructed under these 1930s statutes and extends to stocks, bonds, debentures, evidence of debt, investment contracts, and commodity futures contracts. Also, a "security-based swap agreement" under these statutes captures off-exchange derivatives with a payments component. Both the Securities Act, at 15 U.S.C. § 77b, and the Securities Exchange Act, at 15 U.S.C. § 78c define "securities" and "exchanges." The SEC takes the statutory definition and defines the subdivisions of securities. "Exchanges" (like the New York Stock Exchange) are overseen by the SEC, while "boards of trade" (like the American Stock Exchange) are monitored by the Commodity Futures Trading Commission. The CFTC supervises commodities futures and options trading.

FINRA (the nationwide securities industry self-regulatory organization—SRO—or regulator) is an agent of the SEC for many functions. The SEC has oversight authority and can act without cease, while FINRA is limited in its ability to take direct action. These SEC/FINRA responsibilities are concentrated in six categories. This paper particularly speaks to day trading activities found within one of the SEC/FINRA categories: dealing in securities.

Tax Implications

Taxes - Long-term investors might not hold their assets for more than 365 days, and they can be taxed at a lower rate, typically 15%. Short-term trades are going to be taxed at a higher rate, typically between 24% - 37% (2021).

Keep in mind that depending on how active you are in the market, it will determine how much of your profits will be taxed for Medicare. The IRS breaks this tax down into 3 categories: Non-Professional Traders, Professional Traders, and Professional Traders who have not requested Trader Tax Status.

Non-Professional Traders: These are casual traders who rarely trade and rarely make a profit. They are considered investors in the eyes of the IRS. You are only required to pay long or short-term capital gains tax on the profits resulting from the securities transactions. What is not typically known is that you cannot claim trading losses. This is because the IRS favors long-term investments. Keep in mind that if for some odd reason you only have losses for the year, you can typically only write off my losses up to a maximum of $3,000. If there are still losses for that year that exceeded $3,000, they will be carried forward to the following year. However, these losses don't expire and can be carried forward indefinitely.

Professional Traders with TTS: This is the only group that is allowed to deduct trading losses if they are extensive in that tax year.

If you're a full-time trader, know that there are a few additional considerations you must keep in mind. You will need an Account Statement, Tax document, Form 1214, and Schedule D.

CHAPTER 12

Case Studies and Examples

A third of the reason for a new trader's failure is not seeing the necessary situations. Elite trading tactics touch on nearly 100 real trading situations, some using the author's trades and trading account.

While others are the trading of the thousands of traders the author has worked with over fifteen years. Trading is the art of the subjective. It requires a feel, intuition and sense for the pulse of the markets. In an attempt to upgrade the new trader to a feel for trading for the benefit of his or her equity and ego, on nearly every page I've incorporated pertinent case studies and lots of examples. Each contributes to giving the author in-training an education he or she can take to the bank. Elite trading tactics and strategies are based on a warrior's approach. Most literature on trading is left to the high-stress world of day trading. In Elite Trading Tactics I draw the draw ties on all sorts of trading time frames and vehicles to demonstrate successful, successful trading fronts.

Throughout this book you'll be treated to loads of trading advice drawn from real-life trading scenarios. These illustrate from the trading warriors exploring the front lines ala case study and examples.

Some of the case studies are cleverly mixed with the day trading tales of the author along with plenty borrowed from trading acquaintances during the author's fifteen-year career working with over four thousand traders.

Real-Life Trading Scenarios
Real-life trading scenarios help you to visualize the market environment that traders encounter on a day-to-day basis. The purpose of this section isn't to give a recount of what happened on any given day but rather give examples where traders had to maneuver within their trading time frame. Scenarios range from introductory to advanced, and should provide you with real-world examples of how these tactics are used in the real world.

Overcoming the Odds The S&P 500 had moved in an upward direction and then began to move aggressively in a downwards direction until it reached an important value area. At this important level (1992), the market began to chop around with above-average volumes. There was also a downtrend among the intermediate time frame, which helped confirm that the market was in more than just a slight disturbance in the trading field. This was an intraday trading situation, and the S&P 500 was in an overall bearish condition because it was within a high volume area and the intermediate trend of the 15-minute time frame was in a downtrend.

Using Combination Plays to Lower Trading Costs Introduction: Every Tuesday morning at 8:30 AM, the Building Permits Report is released, and traders expect the market to receive a good volatility push. The strategy for this trade is expected to be a reversal trade in the direction of the primary market trend on Tuesdays only. On the morning the report was released, the S&P 500 was expected to trade to the upside if the Building Permits Report was favorable. If the report was not favorable, the S&P 500 was expected to trade to the downside.

Successful Day Traders

Studying successful day traders allows us to appreciate the various approaches that contribute to trading success. These interviews are consistently interesting, in large part because most day traders have unique trading tactics. Witnessing their honesty about trading is also appealing. In particular, consider the following facets of the Elite trading office strategy: (1) How long the psychology associated with day trading can take to master. (2) "The consistent theme that keeps surfacing is the time and emotional discipline involved to be successful at day trading." (3) Trading edges are quite subjective. The following are the five traits of the Elite trading office identified by these interviews. Clearly, it demonstrates that successful trading is every bit a mindset as well as a specific trading approach.

For day traders to be successful, they need to have a mentality for trading and not a gambling mindset. In conjunction with the excellent interviews that the Elite trading office conducted, a professional psychologist interviewed Elite trading office's swing and position traders. He developed a series of questions and conducted a three-hour interview session. His questions controlled that the swing and position traders had more self-motivation than the average individuals he had been working with up to that point. The results were so interesting that we did a three-hour session with the day traders. The same theme appeared in each of the Elite trading office traders. They had more passion for trading than any other activity: "I wake up in the morning with a smile on my face because I get to trade."

CHAPTER 13

Conclusion and Next Steps

This book has covered thirteen elite trading tactics that, if practiced, will up your game as a day trader of stocks, options, or underlying. Each tactic covered in this book represents an area of technical analysis, trading psychology, trading mechanics, risk management, or market mechanics that elite day traders have an understanding and proficiency in. We have covered measures, peculiar order interaction, trend tail spotting, continuation flag marking, relative volatility index (RVI) divergences, premium crush zones, volatility recalculation post-earnings, position delta metric option positioning, the "Saturday announcement effect," day trading short interest, day trading binary events, avoiding tyranny of compounding through proper portfolio leverage, and day trading the news. We hope the insights here in this book help you trade better; the process of course, is for you to internalize these insights by practicing them in the real world. We would recommend a few resources to continue your learning in these areas. In terms of trading psychology, granulates trading psychology issues in daily bite-size issues that can be quickly assimilated. In the realm of dynamic analytics of markets: for a solid treatment of markets from the classical CTEP perspective.

for quality how-to. The same goes for which serves as a nice desk reference for many aspects covered in this book. On the markets, is admired by many professionals. "The Dow Theory" is the last word in technical analysis for many dow theorists. Further study in dynamic hedging gives "Random Portfolios for evaluating dynamic trading strategies (paper)" and "Analysis of Portfolio Strategies based on options", both by Leland. For market history and breadth, nothing beats Daily Closing Breadth Ratios, by Ron Griess. provides powerful insights into what makes options prices move in Options Made Easy. Those interested in cleaning up bond strategy will find evidence that is also important in this area in "What moves the bond market?" with Howard Cook.

Dewey Parker. Executive Summary

• We have addressed portfolio leverage in each section (including the full discussion of day trading the news in the appendix) to ensure the day trader's portfolio is under- or over-leveraged to the desired position delta metric. • Historically, we have found the best way to stay under-leveraged yet generate exceptional trading profits is to: Beyond a shadow of a doubt, the most important tactic in this paper is ∂-trading. An insight of this nature that is so foundational to one's belief about the world and particularly about trading is rare indeed. When you can do this properly, then how you play your earnings trades can be best left to an optimization exercise that looks at how you can most cost-effectively spread your long and short positions across equities, calls, and puts given your existing positions and order flow assumptions about stocks, the options, and exchange rules. We hope we have whet your appetite in these topics and that you are inspired to continue studying in these areas. Happy trading!

Summary of Key Points

That concludes the guide to Elite Tactics. The main takeaway is that combining option signals with stocks is a form of market synthesis. As usual, buying options alone is like putting money in the garbage can. Selling options works better but can cause you to go broke. Combine indicators to get a better than 50/50 shot at making money.

Market timing with options of a stock ETF is a form of market synthesis. Stocks (ETFs) do one of two things – break to new highs, go sideways, or break to new lows. Meaning a stock (ETF) has a 67% chance of being anything but declining in value. Option market indicators (DITM) have a greater than 50% odds of making money. When used as a trade management tactic, I should have an edge. Identifying where money is flowing and where the rubber meets the road is a solid concept. Traders putting money (and assuming risk) on the edge of the stock price shows more strong hands getting into position where accumulating stock breaks the stock price out of stasis better than indicators that focus on rationalizations. Trading stocks at the moment options are being bought or sold seems to help make the probabilities of resulting profit that much better.

Further Learning Resources

There's no need to be embarrassed if you didn't secure top scores in our trading quizzes. It's just the nature of the beast. Most educators will agree with us on this point: no one is going to be delivering a comprehensive strategy or a comprehensive education in day trading in a $700 package that's accessible to anyone with a computer. Our advice on this front is fairly simple. If you have the time and money available to do so, we recommend considering further education as a trader in addition to learning from online resources, wherever possible. Below are just a few of our favorites:

Further Learning Resources 1. The Pro Package with Trading MasterClass and Quast Futures. We mentioned John Hoagland's book, Trading MasterClass earlier on the page, and we'll mention it again below. Investors tend to purchase an entire package that incorporates not only the book but a variety of other materials that can help in building a comprehensive foundation in trading. If you're interested in TradeGuider VSA software, this is the best deal you can get. However, for traders who are only interested in the books and educational materials, packages are also available that contain nothing but products and materials from Hoagland.